Neighborhood Safari

Bullfrogs

by Martha London

www.focusreaders.com

Focus Readers is distributed by North Star Editions: sales@northstareditions.com | 888-417-0195

Produced for Focus Readers by Red Line Editorial.

Photographs ©: Shutterstock Images, cover, 1, 4, 6, 8, 12, 17, 21 (tadpoles); iStockphoto, 11; Kenneth H. Thomas/Science Source, 15; Dante Fenolio/Science Source, 18; Red Line Editorial, 21 (chart)

Library of Congress Cataloging-in-Publication Data
Names: London, Martha, author.
Title: Bullfrogs / by Martha London.
Description: Lake Elmo, MN : Focus Readers, [2021] | Series: Neighborhood safari | Includes index. | Audience: Grades 2-3
Identifiers: LCCN 2019060255 (print) | LCCN 2019060256 (ebook) | ISBN 9781644933510 (hardcover) | ISBN 9781644934272 (paperback) | ISBN 9781644935798 (pdf) | ISBN 9781644935033 (ebook)
Subjects: LCSH: Bullfrog--Juvenile literature.
Classification: LCC QL668.E27 L66 2021 (print) | LCC QL668.E27 (ebook) | DDC 597.8/92--dc23
LC record available at https://lccn.loc.gov/2019060255
LC ebook record available at https://lccn.loc.gov/2019060256

Printed in the United States of America
Mankato, MN
082020

About the Author

Martha London writes books for young readers. When she's not writing, you can find her hiking in the woods.

Table of Contents

Chapter 1

Near the Water

A bullfrog sits in the grass near a pond. Suddenly, the frog jumps. It catches a **cricket** in its mouth.

Bullfrogs are found in many countries. Some countries have **native** bullfrogs. In other places, bullfrogs were brought by people. The bullfrogs spread in these new areas.

Fun Fact

A group of frogs is called an army.

A Big Frog

Bullfrogs are **amphibians**. They live near water. Bullfrogs are good swimmers. They have webbed feet. Bullfrogs dive deep underwater to escape **predators**.

Bullfrogs use round **eardrums** to hear. Bullfrogs have wide mouths. They have strong back legs. Bullfrogs leap to catch **prey**. They can jump fast and far. Some can go 6 feet (1.8 m) in one hop.

Fun Fact

Bullfrogs can grow up to 8 inches (20 cm) long.

eye

eardrum

back leg

mouth

webbed foot

Chapter 3

Hiding and Hunting

Bullfrogs are green or brown. Their skin color helps them blend in with the things around them. Many bullfrogs live near lakes and ponds.

Bullfrogs hunt at night. They hide and wait. Then they grab prey with their long tongues. Bullfrogs will eat anything that fits in their mouths. They eat insects and crayfish. They even eat other frogs.

earthworm

Croaks and Calls

Bullfrogs are known for making a low-pitched call. Male bullfrogs use this sound to tell other males to stay away. The call also attracts female frogs. Bullfrogs make other sounds, too. One is an alarm call. This call sounds like a squeak. Bullfrogs make this call before jumping into the water.

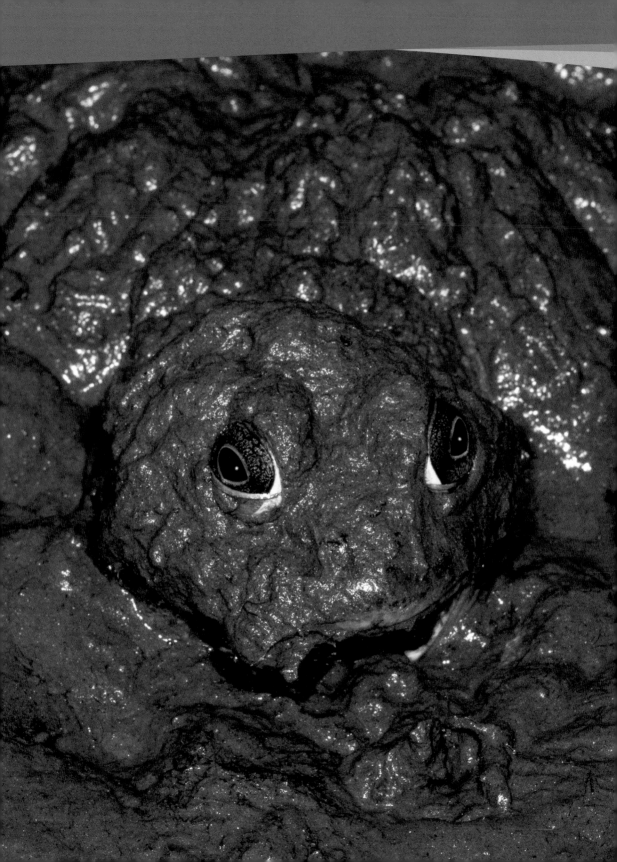

Chapter 4

Bullfrog Behavior

Some bullfrogs live in places that get cold in winter. These bullfrogs **hibernate**. They rest and hide in mud and water.

In spring, female bullfrogs start laying eggs. **Tadpoles** hatch from the eggs. They live in water. The tadpoles taste bad to fish. As a result, many tadpoles survive. They become adults.

Fun Fact

A female bullfrog can lay 20,000 eggs at one time.

Life Cycle

Female bullfrogs lay eggs in water.

Tadpoles hatch from the eggs after a few days.

Bullfrogs live up to nine years in the wild.

The tadpoles live in the water for one to three years.

Small frogs leave the water.

Eventually, tadpoles lose their tails and grow legs.

FOCUS ON
Bullfrogs

Write your answers on a separate piece of paper.

1. Write a sentence describing how bullfrogs hunt.

2. Would you want to hibernate in winter? Why or why not?

3. Where do bullfrogs live?
   A. only in cold places
   B. only in dry places
   C. in countries around the world

4. What might happen if bullfrog tadpoles did not taste bad to fish?
   A. More tadpoles would have tails.
   B. More tadpoles would get eaten by fish.
   C. More tadpoles would survive to become adults.

Answer key on page 24.

Glossary

amphibians
Animals that live partly on land and partly in water.

cricket
An insect that can jump high and make a chirping sound.

eardrums
Patches of skin that vibrate and allow a frog to hear.

hibernate
To rest during cold months to save energy.

native
Originally from a certain place.

predators
Animals that hunt other animals for food.

prey
Animals that are eaten by other animals.

tadpoles
Young frogs and toads that have tails and live only in water.

To Learn More

BOOKS

Albertson, Al. *American Bullfrogs*. Minneapolis: Bellwether Media, 2020.

Kenney, Karen Latchana. *Life Cycle of a Frog*. Minneapolis: Jump!, 2019.

NOTE TO EDUCATORS

Visit **www.focusreaders.com** to find lesson plans, activities, links, and other resources related to this title.

Index

Answer Key: 1. Answers will vary; **2.** Answers will vary; **3.** C; **4.** B